Jenna Plewes

Salt

Indigo Dreams Publishing

First Edition: Salt
First published in Great Britain in 2013 by:
Indigo Dreams Publishing
132 Hinckley Road
Stoney Stanton
Leics
LE9 4LN

www.indigodreams.co.uk

ISBN 978-1-909357-12-9

British Library Cataloguing in Publication Data. A CIP record for this book can be obtained from the British Library.

Designed and typeset in Palatino Linotype by Indigo Dreams.

Cover design by Ronnie Goodyer at Indigo Dreams

Printed and bound in Great Britain by Imprint Academic, Exeter.

Papers used by Indigo Dreams are recyclable products made from wood grown in sustainable forests following the guidance of the Forest Stewardship Council.

*to my mother who loved the sea, the stars
and the quiet earth*

Acknowledgements

Some of these poems have appeared in Labour of Love, Poetry Cornwall, Sarasvati and the Crablines Off The Pier anthology.

CONTENTS

Salt

The Great Sea has set me in motion
Set me adrift
And I move as a weed in the river
The Arch of sky
And mightiness of storms
Encompasses me
And I am left
Trembling with joy.

Aii Aii Eskimo song

Nautilus

In the quiet room
windows yawn and stretch,
curtains beat great white wings
tugging at the tethers.

She leans forward
wide open in the arms of a new day.

The nautilus shell lies
in the humped dunes of the bed
a glistening mouth
chambered in coils of silk.

Chambered in coils of silk
a glistening mouth
in the humped dunes of the bed
the nautilus shell lies
wide open in the arms of a new day.

She leans forward
tugging at the tethers,

curtains beat great white wings
windows yawn and stretch
in the quiet room.

Soul Time

Go early

before anyone's up
there's a lot to carry
stray bits will drop out on the way
sand has a warm touch
sea is a salt kiss.

Let it all go,

wonder at the weight
watch a skin of water flood in
swirl round your feet
take everything with a long sigh.

Wander back

swinging an empty sack
full of possibilities.

Long Shadows

Long shadows creep across the windblown hill
the clouds catch fire, the light will soon be gone
you cannot hold this bird-bright moment still.

When flames die down, the winter air is chill
and water turns to ice before too long,
long shadows creep across the windblown hill.

To catch the grains of time before they spill
or think to build with sun-beams would be wrong
you cannot hold this bird-bright moment still.

Though some will strive and drive themselves until
they reach the peak no one yet walked upon
long shadows creep across the windblown hill.

Go roller-coast the cresting surf, fulfil
the dreams you have, soar while the wind is strong
you cannot hold this bird-bright moment still.

Some borrow time, or lose it. You must fill
your life, to be where you belong
long shadows creep across the windblown hill
you cannot hold this bird-bright moment still.

Going Under

Hand over hand
I let myself down
under the surface
of a dark sea.
A thread unwinds
finer than thought
loop
by loop
by loop.
Strange beings
feel their way
through
the fissures
of my brain
memories stir
like weeds
in the tide.

Hours ripple over the seabed,
send up puffs of sand
that settle like grit on my eyelids.

A cold current
washes over my skin
lifts away the sediment
shadows tug at my eyes
I pull myself
hand over hand
up to the light.

Beware, Thin Ice

Tread lightly
move forward
with infinite care
see spider threads
of black water
hear the creak and crack
of the ice
as it shifts
with your weight.

The smooth cold surface
tells no story till you kneel
and look at what's embedded there,

dreams
hopes and
sorrows
locked in
frozen against the pain
that comes when the ice melts
and the weeping begins.

The Final Session

Punctual you come for one last session
take out your notes
spilling the words
soft as surf on a distant shore

smoothing the final page
you close the file
and walk into the quiet afternoon.

Standing in the falling tide,
a skin of water
healing the troubled sand
I think of you, and wish you well.

Sandbank

Muscles ripple under the skin of the sea
as it surges forward
then slips back.
A pale scattering
lies across the bulge of the bay
like scurf on the shoulders of a funeral suit.

A deep fold of sand
hard as the rib of a whale
lies under the waves
a current licks along it
mouths at the bodies of swimmers
when they come close.

Survivors let the current take them
swim into the pain
wait through the slow unpicking of the hours
until they drift into the shallows
beyond the headland
where the sand bears no familiar prints.

Sea Glass

Spinning sunlight
it arcs, bottle-green blue
shatters on a blind rock face
sprays the shingle with splinters,
slivers that cut deep to the bone
glitter and scream 'don't touch'

the sea takes them
transforms them
churning surf
smoothes the cutting edge
softens bright transparency
to cloudy beauty.

I sift my sea glass hoard
to find a milk-white shard
peach-pelted now, rounded as a sigh,
hold it close,
painless against my heart.

Miscarriage

All week an east wind
tramples the horizon
rips the sea to shreds

the bay is quiet
waves fingering the shore

a dune swells at the tide-line
sand moulded firm
each day a fuller curve

but now the wind veers west
hurls its fury on the beach
claws the sand away

and in its place it leaves
a waste of bladder-wrack, and weed
clotted with rubbish, thick with trash

and at the water's edge I stand and grieve.

Healing

Wind rasps the sea's frail skin,
spume-blown torn dressings
unravel the swell,
shadows spread like purple bruises.

Curtains at the open window
snap and crack like full set sails
her hands wrinkled as windswept water
pleat the restless coverlet
the room breathes slowly,

far beyond her gaze
a soft rain soothes the waves
blurs the razor sharp horizon
the cutting edge of pain.

Abused

Far away
something below the surface stirs
ripples swell into waves

gathering power they come steadily closer
muscling white knuckled fists
growing higher and higher, spitting foam

until roaring, they abandon all control
crash down, splinter in a mess of spume,
and fling a torn sheet of beaten water up the beach.

After the storm
the waves are calm
wheedling their way through the wreckage
sliding down the beach

while she picks up shattered plastic, broken wood
and with careful fingers tries to salvage
the torn netting tangled with weed

believing something can be saved.

Ebb Tide

I brought flowers from the garden
to remind you of home
roses, honeysuckle, pinks,
in a jam-jar of water,

found you clenched tight as a fist
curled round your pain
lost in a thundercloud of pillows
out of reach.

They say you watched the flowers
as you faded
and the water ebbed away.

Albatross

The sea unrolls a creased blind
white streaks appear and disappear
as it moves in the wind
random thoughts shine through rips in the cloth
blink and are gone
before my mind can grasp them.

Something below the surface
illuminates everything.

A solitary gull quarters the oceans
snagged with dreams.

Requiem for Jo

I

No one witnessed it
an ordinary day cut to the quick.

A stone cold bed
an empty plate
an open book
scream in the deafening silence
on the windowsill
a blood red geranium
blooms defiantly.

Don't search here for answers
or rummage through a litany of pain
close the door now
but leave the window open
to the healing night
an infinity of stars
above the breathing sea
she loved so much.

II

You were never really free
the long string let you take the heady up-draught
soar with the windblown gulls
but only so far and so long
then the downward pull of the past
dragged you back
to the clinging mud and the lonely dark.

III

So we lit you a candle,
and set it afloat
your light
taken by wind and tide
moves steadily out from the darkening shore
to the gleaming sea.

R.I.P. Richard

A coast clawed and bitten
endlessly sea stormed
cliffs speckled with a scattering of gulls
bedded in sea pink cushions

the long drop to unquiet surf
frothing rotten teeth
snarling below

a narrow shingle beach
clings to the cliffs
with no path down

at low tide
all that remains
wedged between rocks

your broken watch
glints in the fitful sun,
hands stopped at 10 past 6

The Boardwalk

Above the tree line
the wind peels back heather and moss
leaving the pulpy shoulder of the hill
raw and wet

a boardwalk two railway sleepers wide
lays a careful finger
over the broken skin of the pass

figures lurch across
hit by gusts that catch them unawares
fighting to shake them off.

I've travelled there and know
there is no easy way through grief.

Geometry

Diagonals of rain intersect the line
pencilled between sky and sea.

A buzzard circles its compass on the clouds
followed by gulls taking the diameter.

Fat raindrops draw concentric rings
on the wet paving squares

before the bonfire's smoke rag
erases everything.

Bled White

White-faced the sky
slumps over a pallid sea
leached of all colour

a convalescent day
drained of energy
turned inward on itself
against the cold

when sorrow
steals in unannounced
through a half open door.

Shapeshifting

On a still grey day it squats
a warty toad on a pewter plate
watching the waves

moonlight picks at it
a lone black tooth in a glistening mouth

storms battle its armoured body
tank tracks bedded in sand.

A black rock
gripped in the jaws of the bay

watches me
watch your face
across the breakfast table,

unreadable,

and out of reach.

Decree Absolute

A sky white as frostbitten flesh
hangs over a steel-plated sea
cold-soldered at the margin.

Seascape January 2011
abstract in monochrome
white and grey with fine black horizontal

on the doormat underneath
an official brown envelope.

Thaw

Winter has sleep in its eyes
misting all things
a stonewashed sea fades,
the horizon blurred by a dusty finger

headlands dissolve layer by layer
smudging a tired sky
inland the stream trickles through sedge
stiff and brown as three-day stubble,

a softening is taking place
of things held tight with cold
all things are loosening
unfurling into Spring

and somewhere deep inside
a fist of ice opens its fingers,
flooding my face with the taste of salt.

Sinister Tree

Two days ago
I came across a trainer
yesterday a sneaker, caught amongst the rocks
this morning, full of sand, I found a shoe

all different, all left feet.

Twelve months on, I find
another shoe wedged in the rocks
today a sandal at the high tide mark

all different, all left feet.

Somewhere there is a sinister tree
with lopsided limbs
that each day bears a single fruit,

from time to time, carried by wind and wave
a sodden harvest, salty and unexpected,
washes onto the beach.

Facing the Wind

Pushing against the wind
I climb the hill
the scarred sea
at my back.

It's a hard climb
thorn trees scabbed with lichen
grip the slope with twisted hands
carved by the wind
they have the tempered beauty
of those whose lives are spent
walking into the wind.

Holdfast

Quite a night by the look of it,
seaweed everywhere,
brown shoelaces in impossible sandy knots
leather belts, flounced and ruffled sashes,
silken scarves
left at high water mark now the party's over,

but look more closely,
torn fingers
severed hands
of rockweed and kelp
litter the sand.

While the waves writhed and twisted overhead
the tide reached down
tore them loose
dumped them like displaced persons
on the smooth-faced sand
and went away.

Symphony

It begins quietly at first
a snare-drum
of feet pacing through dry grass

rounding the headland
a swell of organ chords
as the wind gusts up the valley

spiralling above this base rhythm
snatches of birdsong,
lark, stonechat, and finch

in a rustle of thorn trees
hunkered in the cleft
between bracken brown hills

then as the sounds of sea and birdsong fade away
the stream runs its fingers over the piano keys
in a shimmer of broken chords

now the sea comes into view,
the surf returns, the wind gusts,
the orchestra plays,
the sun comes up.

Mist Nets

On the cliff top
trees cower
backs to a wind
that rubs them raw
a lane burrows
through gorse
into a valley spread like a wide green lap.

This is where he hangs his mist nets
as light comes and the migrant birds arrive.

He untangles the tiny bodies
in his huge hands
feels the frantic heartbeats
like quivers at the corner of a mouth
trying not to cry
then tagged and registered
he lets them go
watches them beat into the wind
caught on a line his keen eyes cannot see
that reels them in.

Power Cut

Gulls flick past like paper darts.

A blank sky waits for something to happen.

Leaves torn from my notebook
drift into piles round my chair.

A flock of finches come to the feeder.

Power lines score an empty page.
Nothing comes through.

On the Rampage

The wind is driving the sea crazy
tearing the tops off the waves
driving them up the beach
forcing them into the rocks
where they mill around
like cornered sheep.

Dirty white slavers the cliffs
and far inland gobbets of foam
catch on the bushes
lie quivering in the grass
fleeing the war of water and wind.

Spindrift

Waves suck and surge
in the heave of the sea
tongue the gaps between broken teeth

flecks of foam hover and reel
like foraging bees
tremble in tussocks of sweeping grass

sea mist turns bracken to rust
hangs beads on the bramble wire
rubs wind-whipped skin with salt

spinning and drifting
up the empty valley
where no one lives.

On a Falling Tide

After a restless night
the sea has quietened

waves move over the beach
with indifferent ease
make no sound as they retreat
pulling the sand taut
tucked in tight to the cliffs

seaweeds slide in the yawn of the sea
a shoulder rolls upwards
a thin arm flails
wisps of hair catch on the rocks

torn from their moorings
they float in the current
till the waves gather them up
lay them in tidy rows
at the high water mark

while in a hospital ward
a bright wren of a woman
in the end bed
gazes over a sea of bedcovers
to the horizon.

Lost Summer

Storm over
the sea sleeps

weed fingers the shallows
catspaws ruffle the surface
flicker across a dreaming face

a mess of plastic
seaweed, tangled trash
lies at high watermark

lost amongst the litter
a sodden paperback
a sunscreen tube, a broken body-board

the memory of summer's idleness
a lapis sea under a cloudless sky.

Springtime on the Moor

Gorse flares and sizzles
in a flood of bluebells
washing around rocks crusted with lichen.

Perched on warm granite
in a blue-gold haze of sunlight and birdsong
I freeze frame the moment
before it joins cloud shadows
racing across the moor.

Happiness

Wash your hands in bluebells
hold them in the heat of the gorse
peel off winter's heavy coat
and run into the satin-sheeted sea.

Amnio

Floating on my back
rocked by the waves
I am wrapped in a liquid skin
lulled by the suck and surge of the sea
a heartbeat older than breath.

Spellbound

Lit by a full moon
roof tiles are shining fish-scales
trees a fretwork of jet
pale grasses cobweb the paths
the garden lies cold as death.

Between the hills
the sea quivers
scarred with light,
nothing moves

through the silence
steals the rustle of dreams
on the dark sands of sleep.

Lying in a Hot Tub Watching Shooting Stars

Moonrise will be late tonight
swaddled in warmth
we lie in the dark
waiting for them

darting like fish
they come
from all directions
flashing past
before eyes can trap them

sparking
      fizzing
            vanishing,

we spin through a ricochet of stars

                    unscathed.

In Memory of Hiroshima

Each year we gather on the bridge at dusk
as the rooks leave the mudflats

a swirl of charred fragments stirred by the evening breeze
harsh cries tearing the peace to shreds
till they spiral like smoke to the distant woods.

As the light fades we carry the candle boats
down to the shore, set them afloat
watch the lanterns drawn seawards

by the falling tide
till pinpricks in the darkness, one by one their light dies
and we turn away.

Eclipse

The wind has died
the sky hangs motionless
a dead world gnaws at the sun
daylight bleeds away

songbirds fall silent
cattle no longer feed
dogs crouch mute
skin prickles.

Darkness rises like floodwater
filling eyes, ears, mouths
we shrink to a heartbeat
a shallow breath

second by slow second,
the sun heaves back the dark
seals up the hairline crack
one more time.

Scoured Sand

Low tide is best
a glorious emptiness
washed clean of words
scoured of clogged ideas
stretches luxuriously beneath a quiet sky

the sea, withdrawn and mindless
churns countless grains of sand
waiting moonstruck to turn
flood rock pool and cave

the calm shores
of my mind.

Unexpected Gift

iridescent foam
clustered rainbows
on wet sand.

Sweet Water

In the top field
where the grass is young and green
there are underground springs

years ago clay pipes
collected the water
hid it in the wide lap of the valley
took it down to the sea

sweet water drowned
in the waves.

Then something broke through
unearthed the pipes
tossed the fragments aside
like scattered vertebrae.

Now water finds a wide new way
like someone opening a gate
leaving behind the hidden hurts
doubts and buried dreams

to walk in sunlight
under a generous sky.

Teasing

Ankle deep
she faces down the waves
seduced by the pull of the water
on her naked feet.

The rollers swagger in
sinking into smiles
unroll their bolts of silk
tangle them round her legs

tug them back
clawing the sand from under her toes
race away from her dizzying eyes
and staggering feet.

The shouldering sea
speeds towards her
runs cold hands up to her knees
swirls away triumphant
as she runs laughing up the beach.

The Stream

The stream runs like a long limbed girl
out towards the sea
crimped and tangled strands
spread out across the shore
red gold in the low evening light

sinking in surf
where wave and water meet
I watch the sea take the sun
to a pearl grey bed

climb the hill home
to fire-lit loving
your hair loose over your breasts
tangling my fingers
in its rippling stream.

The Midas Touch

The horizon melts
in the gape of the sun
clouds catch fire
gunmetal sea turns to gold

rocks tear the waves in tinselled shreds,
a gold-leaf skin wrinkles the surf
waves sticky as honey
gloop my feet

a fly in amber
I wait for the sun to drown.

Gannets

The cliff is white with nesting gulls
each with a single egg
nested in yolk yellow feet.

Year on year they come
to the same ledge
to the same mate
predictable as the tide

the sky explodes with birds
they slice the surface of the sea
write delicate calligraphy
on a deep blue bowl

a beatitude of birds
free wheeling a sunlit cycle

earth bound each to each.

Summer Children

Sun bleached sands
forget-me-not skies
seagulls laughing in the wind

water lustrous as ancient glass
violet shadowed where tiny fish
dart through bladderwrack forests

my children, bare bottomed and free
wander in seaweed gardens
where anemone fingers stroke their hands

the cold tide rises
clouds blur the line
between now and forever.

Sunrise

The valley lies in shadow,
the sea a pewter plate
wedged between crumpled cliffs
blackened rocks denting the rim.

Dunlin forage the foreshore
oystercatchers pick their way
across the beach on pink legs
orange beaks probing the sand.

A gull high on the rocks
flings a knife-edged cry
into the clear air
cutting away the sorrows of the night.

Slowly the sun rises
and a huge smile spreads
across the bracken-bearded slopes
of this weather-beaten land.

Indian Summer

Today the air is sharp as a crisp apple

sheep flow through the bracken
a thin stream of milk in a bronze bowl
mushrooms push bald heads through the grass
puffballs swell up like bullfrogs

far off a crinkled tinfoil sea scatters the light

on the cliff top path a mile away
humpbacked walkers glide like cardboard cut-outs
it's so still we catch their conversation
a mooring line flung across the valley,

the sun-bleached bench is warm against our backs
the coffee hot and bitter-sweet as an Autumn day.

Wild

A solitary buzzard carves its image
on the fingerpost
that points the way to the beach

watches the dog quartering the field
turns its head
as the dog passes
beneath the plinth.

I inch closer
offer my heart on the palm of my hand,

long before I reach the place
the hawk snares the wild sky
writes its name on the high white clouds.

Salt

On the cliff top we taste the sea in winter
the birdfeeder's chain turns black
iron bleeds rust on the paving stones
windows gather a haze of salt
the leaves of the rose bushes scorch

but when it turns warm
the breeze is full of the sea's breath
smelling of sun bleached sheets
and summer's idleness.

I trace your body with my tongue
taste salt in each loved fold and crease
rise and fall in the swell of your sleep
the ceaseless conversation of the sea
soft in my ears.

Bird Watching

Two buzzards are swinging the sun
in a deep blue sheet
that lifts and falls
furling and unfurling in the breeze

and when they spin away
the ground lurches under my feet
I'm dizzy as a birthday child
tossed in a blanket.

Beyond the Comfort Zone

Go out beyond the breaking waves
where the pregnant sea
heaves and strains
till the perfect wave is born

then take it, ride it
all the way

(safe in the shallows
I've never gone out of my depth)

only in dreams I ride the perfect wave
and waking, vow while there's still time
I'll venture farther out.

Flight

The gale is ripping the top off the world,
the sun laughs in my face
tosses me in the air

spiralling higher and higher
I see the cove, a cup of milk
tipped in the sea
the two valleys pleating
the faded rug of the moor
its granite-worn holes
streams like broken silver threads
scattered shadows like tufts of wool.

Clouds snuff out the sun
I open my eyes
high overhead a hawk hangs
motionless.

Seeing

Somewhere out there the sea
sighs and turns in its sleep
hidden by a thick white fullness
that is an emptiness
I cannot tear apart
to see behind or peer ahead.

My narrow lens
sharpens everything

grasses bend like fishing rods
baited with water
tiny flowers
burn with blue flames
an empty bird's egg, eyelid thin
holds a lake of milk

while a snail waves its eye-stalks
like groping fingers in the dark.

Waves

Count them
the seventh will be the highest
it will stream over the beach
taking you by surprise
the seventh child of a seventh child

a hugeness under the ocean
draws the sea into its lungs
breathes out these great translucent hills
that fold and spill
fold and spill

it reaches out watery hands
smoothing the shallows
spreads a cobwebbed shawl
of Shetland lace
fine-drawn as through a wedding ring
and wraps you in its timelessness.

The Abundance of Emptiness

Why does emptiness matter so much?
It's not the lack of anything

it's a silent offering,
untying the knots in my head
prizing my fingers apart
removing the worry stones

it wells up in the deep pool of time
spills over drop by slow drop into my careful hands

it's brim-full of space
the moulded flesh of sun-warmed dunes,
the crests and hollows of the desert's skin
seas that soak up the blueness of the sky
the vault of heaven that hauls me from the earth.

It's not the lack of anything
that frees my eyes to see beyond the seeing
all things connect, nothing to fear in that.

Indigo Dreams Publishing
132, Hinckley Road
Stoney Stanton
Leicestershire
LE9 4LN
www.indigodreams.co.uk